snapshot·picture·library

RAINFOREST ANIMALS

snapshot·picture·library

RAINFOREST ANIMALS

FOG CITY

PRESS

Published by Fog City Press,
a division of Weldon Owen Inc.
415 Jackson Street
San Francisco, CA 94111 USA
www.weldonowen.com

WELDON OWEN INC.
Group Publisher, Bonnier Publishing Group John Owen
President, Chief Executive Officer Terry Newell
Senior Vice President, International Sales Stuart Laurence
Vice President, Sales and New Business Development Amy Kaneko
Vice President, Publisher Roger Shaw
Vice President, Creative Director Gaye Allen
Managing Editor Karen Perez
Assistant Editor Sonia Vallabh
Art Director Bret Hansen
Designer Andreas Schueller
Design Assistant Kevin Yuen
Production Director Chris Hemesath
Production Manager Michelle Duggan
Color Manager Teri Bell

Text Karen Perez
Introduction Barbara Vivian Rogers
Picture Research Brandi Valenza

A WELDON OWEN PRODUCTION
© 2008 Weldon Owen Inc.

ISBN: 978-1-74089-747-1

10 9 8 7 6 5 4 3 2
2011 2012

Printed by Tien Wah Press in Singapore.

The rainforests of the world are special places. The trees here are "the lungs of the world," providing much of the oxygen we breathe.

Under the filtered sunlight, bright birds, monkeys, frogs, and butterflies are at home in the leafy canopies.

Some of the world's strangest animals live here, like birds with beaks half as big as their bodies and reptiles that can change color whenever they feel like it!

Come explore this spectacular green world.

Rainforests
are filled with
colorful birds.

There are birds with horns, like the cassowary, and birds with fancy feathers, like the harpy eagle and the red-crested turaco.

And toco toucans, with their exotic, brightly colored beaks.

Macaws make their home in
the rainforest trees, far away
from predators.

Chameleons make their home in the rainforest, too. They can change the color of their skin to match their surroundings or to stand out, any time they like. Imagine that!

Colorful lizards and snakes find homes in the undergrowth, amongst the fallen leaves.

Tree snakes blend
into the greenery
of the rainforest
leaves, curling
themselves around
hidden branches.

A brown snake,
a bright-green
boa, and a viper
are just a few
of the different
kinds of snakes
that live in
rainforests.

South America
is home to
many rainforest-
dwelling tree
frogs like
these ones
peeking out
from the moist
undergrowth.

Frogs like the moist air of the rainforest and finding dark places to hide.

Brightly colored frogs of the
Amazonian rainforest can have
powerful poison in their skin.

Poison frogs don't make their own poison. They get it from the food that they eat and store it in their skin. This poison is toxic to predators, so they don't make a very tasty meal!

Rainforests are filled with bugs that are unlike any others around the world. They are curious to look at, but watch out for their spikes!

There are beautiful
bugs in the
rainforest, too.

Butterflies like the humidity of the rainforest. Their bright patterns fill the trees with color.

Rainforest
mammals—
orangutans,
anteaters, and
white-handed
gibbons—
are some of
the world's
endangered
animals.

Endangered rainforest mammals can
be as small and timid as the tarsier or
as heavy and slow as a sloth.

Endangered tigers like to roam the rainforest. Their golden fur and black stripes look beautiful as they move through the greenery.

Some animals
have favorite
branches where
they like to
perch and enjoy
the view below.

Lemurs come in many colors. Here is a red-ruffed lemur, enjoying some rainforest sunshine.

The rainforest is home to many monkeys, including golden lion tamarins and woolly monkeys.

Gold, white, black, red— rainforest monkeys' fur and faces come in all sorts of colors!

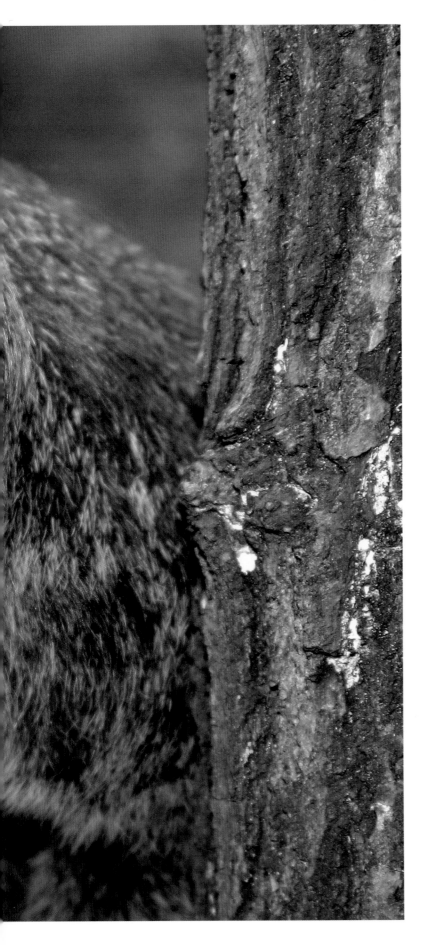

White-faced sakis
are fast moving and
shy. They spend
most of their time
up in the trees.

Tapirs are strange animals that look like a blend between an elephant and a pig.

The great gorillas
of Africa prefer
to sit in the
tall grasses.

The rare okapi is the giraffe's only cousin. It has stripes like a zebra's on its legs.

Like this jaguar, all rainforest animals are awesome sights in the wild. We can help keep it that way and protect rainforests by caring for the environment. So let's get started!

 Chinese Water Dragon	Chameleon	Barred Monkey Frog
Scarlet Ibis	Collared Forest Gecko	Amazon Leaf Frog
Three-Toed Sloth	Brown Vine Snake	Red Back Poison Frog
Hyacinth Macaws	Iguana	Granular Poison Frog
Southern Cassowary	Green Tree Python	Dyeing Poison Frog
Harpy Eagle	Brown Snake	Tropical Harvestman
Red-Crested Turaco	Emerald Tree Boa	Spiny Bush Cricket
Toco Toucan	Temple Viper Snake	Tailless Whip Scorpion
Scarlet Macaw	Red-Eyed Tree Frog	Blue Butterfly
Hyacinth and Scarlet Macaws	Map Tree Frog	Painted Jezebel Butterfly

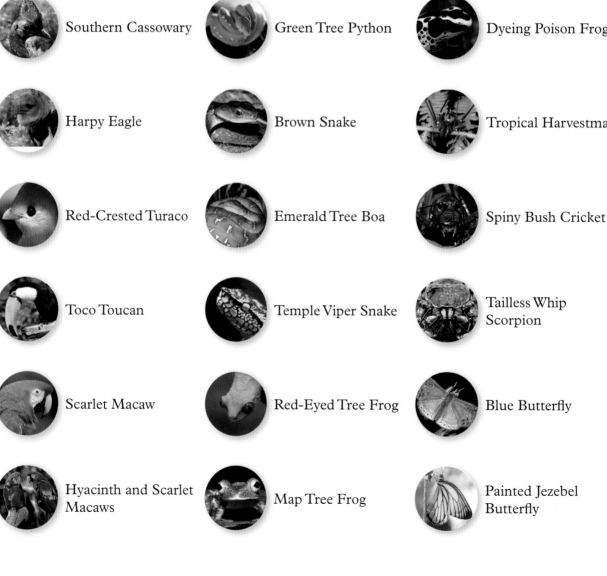

Indian Leaf Butterfly

 Matschie's Tree Kangaroo

 Brazilian Tapir

 Malachite Butterfly

 White-Cheek Gibbon

 Asian Tapir

 Orangutans

 Red Ruffed Lemur

 Brazilian Tapir

 Southern Tamandua Anteater

 Golden Lion Tamarin

 Western Lowland Gorilla

 White-Handed Gibbon

 Woolly Monkey

 Okapi

 Tarsier

 Black-Capped Squirrel Monkey

 Okapi

 Two-Toed Sloth

 White-Cheeked Gibbon

 Jaguar

 Bengal Tiger

 Red Uakari Monkey

 Mandrill

 South American Coatis

 White-Faced Saki

ACKNOWLEDGMENTS

Weldon Owen would like to thank the following people for their assistance in the production of this book: Lori Cockerill, Lucie Parker, Phil Paulick, and Heather Stewart.

CREDITS

All images courtesy of Shutterstock except, the cover and pages 6, 15, and 64 courtesy of iStockphoto.